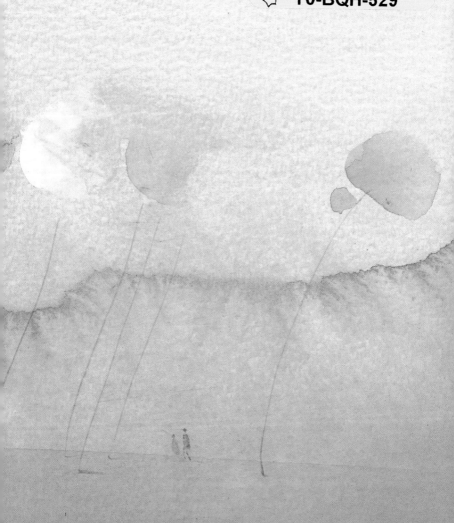

The Country
Flower Companion

The Country
Flower Companion

Tricia Guild
Text by Nonie Niesewand

CollinsPublishersSanFrancisco
A Division of HarperCollins*Publishers*

First published in USA in 1994 by
Collins Publishers San Francisco
1160 Battery Street
San Francisco CA 94111

First published in 1994 by Mitchell Beazley
an imprint of Reed Consumer Books Limited
Michelin House, 81 Fulham Road, London SW3 6RB
and Auckland, Melbourne, Singapore and Toronto

Photography by David Montgomery
Illustrations by David Holmes

Library of Congress Cataloging-in-Publication Data

Guild, Tricia.
       The country flower companion / Tricia Guild ; text by Nonie
Niesewand.
            p.   cm -- (Country companion series)
       Includes index.
       ISBN 0-00-255365-1
       1. Flower arrangement. 2. Flowers. I. Niesewand, Nonie.
       II. Title. III. Series.
    SB449.G83 1994
    745.92--dc20   93-20762
                                                         CIP

Produced by Mandarin
Printed and bound in China

CONTENTS

Introduction   6

SHADES OF THE COUNTRY

Red   10

Pink   14

Yellow   18

Blue   22

Purple   26

Green   28

White   30

Mixed   34

THE COUNTRY GARDEN

Scents of the Country   40

Wild & Garden Flowers   44

Foliage   48

THE ART OF COMPOSITION

Containers   54

Index   62

INTRODUCTION

I can think of nothing that will bring a setting alive more immediately than flowers. Nor anything that offers us a more spontaneous means of arranging the different areas we live in with greater interest and imagination. Sensitively arranged, cut flowers can transform and continually refresh interiors with their natural beauty. The way that flowers look when grouped together in various color combinations is the beginning of creative flower design. The flower arranger can see instantly how colors react together: all you do is take a bunch of stems, set them in a container, stand back and observe the effect. If necessary, remove colors that offend, break up drifts of the same color with leaves or flowers of a different hue, or inject sharp contrast. This book is full of ideas for arranging across the color spectrum and suggests ways to combine diverse textures offered by leaves, stems, grasses and petals, and highlight the magical quality of scent.

Right: A glazed vase filled with a casual display of ranunculus (Ranunculus), euphorbia (Euphorbia robbiae), 'Peach Blush' lilies (Lilium 'Peach Blush') and spiky hosta (Hosta) leaves.

Shades of the Country

RED

Red can be double trouble for flower arrangers striving to harmonize colors. There are two principle groups, crimson and vermilion, and mixing the two in equal proportions can be disastrous, as they will war with each other. Crimson, which is a deep red tinged with blue, belongs with carmine and magenta; while vermilion, which leans toward orange, includes cinnabar and scarlet. Using red successfully in a mixed bunch depends upon picking the right shade – either blue-tinged or yellow-tinged – to go with the other colors in the group. A monochrome arrangement of reds can be enlivened by adding a contrasting shade of red as an accent. A dozen red roses may be a declaration of an admirer, but it says

Below: Bells of Ireland (Moluccella laevis), St John's wort (Hypericum) and gerberas (Gerbera).

Right: Red roses are boldly keyed in to match a crimson pail. The full-strength reds are undiluted by the white and pink roses in the same bunch.
Below: A dish with an artful arrangement of pink and red gerberas and a spray of St John's wort.

more about your style if you add a jolt of, perhaps, creamy pink roses. Employing red in arrangements takes both confidence and tact as it is an advancing color which never retires shyly in a corner. Whether the color reigns supreme in a single-stem vase or contrasts with other hues in a mixed bunch, red will always hold the eye. It is easier by far to combine a vibrant red with a restrained hue than with another of equal strength. Nevertheless, a brilliant and fearless pairing can look stunningly beautiful if you get it right. With the crimsons of cyclamen (Cyclamen), anemones (Anemone) or flowering crab apple (Malus), deep purple foliage makes a rich accompaniment – for example, the velvet-textured leaves of sage (Salvia), purple basil (Ocimum basilicum) or weigela (Weigela). The hot, bright reds of certain tulips (Tulipa), carnations (Dianthus), dahlias (Dahlia), geraniums (Pelargonium), poppies (Papaver) and peonies (Paeonia) team well with silver-gray foliage – gray will not alter adjacent hues, only intensify them. Fiery reds advance out of their background – an effect you can emphasize by choosing dark-green leaves, which will make the reds glow like jewels.

PINK

Pinks offer the flower arranger a host of shades: at one end of the scale pink overlaps with yellow to produce gradations of color to which we give fruit names such as peach and apricot. At the other end of the scale pink fuses with blue and purple to form delicate mauve. Blooms such as the 'Floribunda' rose (*Rosa* 'Floribunda') and some types of gladioli (*Gladiolus*) and gerbera daisies (*Gerbera*) exhibit the warm, peaceful shades of apricots and salmon pinks. These gentle pastels blend particularly well with creams and are complemented by slate-blue such as the gunmetal cider gum (*Eucalyptus gunnii*). In the country garden, mauve flowers are often sweet-smelling, for example, lavender (*Lavandula*), lilac (*Syringa*) and stocks (*Matthiola*) lend heady summer fragrance to a spray of cut flowers, while during the dark winter months, highly scented pink and mauve hyacinths (*Hyacinthus*) may be grown indoors from bulbs. When mixing different pinks, keep the tones closely related and use foliage to heighten or deepen the effect. Pale pinks massed together tend to lose definition, so copy nature and give them a ruff of dark-green leaves. You can emphasize yellow-pinks

Right: A magenta bowl complements pink azaleas (Rhododendron) and alstroemeria (Alstroemeria).
Below: Michaelmas daisies (Aster) with dahlia (Dahlia) buds provide a cheerful composition.

Below: Pink and white hydrangeas (Hydrangea) are mixed with flat-topped Joe Pye weed (Eupatorium purpureum), pink tassels of bridewort (Spiraea salicifolia) and blue love-in-a-mist (Nigella damascena).

and blue-pinks with gray foliage such as senecio *(Senecio)* or silvery ornamental artichoke *(Cynara scolymus)* leaves. Place grasses and seedheads among pink Michaelmas daisies *(Aster)* to accentuate their meadow-sweet freshness. The hot pinks that edge toward orange, for instance azaleas *(Rhododendron)* or peonies *(Paeonia),* blend happily with bright greens such as spurge *(Euphorbia)*, whereas dark green leaves make pale pinks appear redder. The cool pinks that are linked

Above: Clusters of pink blooms complement these spotted vases.

Above: Pale pink hydrangea heads lend a splash of soft color against a collection of fruitwood carvings, containers and old books.

with blue pigments harmonize with mauve and purple, such as heather *(Erica)* on a misty moorland or sweet peas *(Lathyrus odoratus)* on a summer day. Although less emphatic, these cool pinks evoke the cottage garden, since many of the oldest species of flowers are pink – from roses to carnations. For generous displays of pink blooms, early-flowering cherry blossom or lacecap hydrangeas *(Hydrangea)*, that turn pink in an alkaline soil, and mountainous froths of rhododendron *(Rhododendron)* can be cut in great armfuls to make a bold indoor display.

YELLOW

Gold or yellow blooms are always glittering, never dull. The sunflower *(Helianthus)* radiates vitality in its sunburst shape. But equally cheerful are the yellow flowers that come in less symbolic forms, for instance the gilded trumpets of the day lily *(Hemerocallis)* or clusters of fluffy mimosa *(Acacia dealbata)*. Plumes of golden rod *(Solidago)* and spires of yellow snapdragon *(Antirrhinum majus)* seem to reflect the lengthening rays of afternoon sun. Such clear yellow can fill a room with summery brightness. Creamy yellow primulas *(Primula auricula)* and hosts of golden daffodils *(Narcissus)* and meadow buttercups *(Ranunculus acris)* herald the arrival of spring in northern climes. Later, come yellow shrub roses *(Rosa)*, flag irises *(Iris)* and, toward the close of summer, St John's wort *(Hypericum)*.

Below: Yellow mimosa (Acacia dealbata) and yarrow (Achillea) gleam in a scrubbed pine pail.

Right: A loose spray of daffodils (Narcissus).
Below: A glowing marriage of yellow and green.

Above: Orange montbretia (Montbretia) rises above geranium (Pelargonium) leaves. Both share the same yellow pigment and the arrangement harmonizes with a luminous, sunny brightness.

In winter, jasmine *(Jasminum)* lends a sweet fragrance which becomes stronger indoors and wallflowers *(Cheiranthus)* placed in a warm room give off a delectable citron smell. Variegated green-and-yellow foliage is invaluable for creating harmoniously patterned compositions. Suitable ingredients for dappled effects are variegated hollies *(Ilex)*, hostas *(Hosta)*, stems of lemony dogwood *(Cornus)* and ivies *(Hedera)*. Yellows contrast particularly well with violets and purples. As one of many variations on this theme, try combining pale yellow primroses *(Primula vulgaris)* with sprigs of weigela *(Weigela)* and take clippings of purple-leaved smoke tree *(Cotinus)* leaf. A posy using a more restricted palette can be made from 'Harvest Moon' carnations *(Dianthus)*, sunny orange marigolds *(Calendula officinalis)*, russet Peruvian lilies *(Alstroemeria)* and dark-eyed rudbeckia *(Rudbeckia)*; to bind the arrangement use lime green leaves of the tobacco plant *(Nicotiana)*.

Above: Gray senecio (Senecio) makes the hue of neighboring crocosmia (Crocosmia) more intense.
Below: An impromptu nosegay catches the sun.

Another approach is to use yellow or fiery orange flowers to provide an accent in an assorted bunch. Strong yellows and orange are never pale or peaceful and appear to leap forward, instantly grabbing attention with their luminosity. The gleam of a golden lily *(Lilium)* or a lovely curvy stemmed crown imperial *(Fritillaria imperialis)* makes an effective focal point mixed with foliage, or blooms of violet blue .

BLUE

People who say that blue is a cold color have forgotten the gentle blue of a midsummer sky. That fresh, summery blue is sunny rather than chilling. Forget-me-nots *(Myosotis)* and love-in-a-mist *(Nigella damascena)* have the same quality of light and warmth. Nature offers the flower arranger all sorts of shades of blue – from the strong hues of cornflowers *(Centaurea cyanus)* and gentians *(Gentiana)* to the softer array of lupins *(Lupinus)*, delphiniums *(Delphinium)* and scabious *(Scabiosa)*. Blues are as infinite as the sky in their ability to deepen or lighten according to the petals' bloom. Variations on blue within a single family, such as

Below: Deep blue delphiniums (Delphinium) mixed with a gray bud of whitebeam (Sorbus aria) and ice-green guelder rose (Viburnum opulus).

Right: Bold blue hydrangea (Hydrangea) heads.
Below: Less is more in this diminutive bouquet of delphinium blooms and reed-like grasses.

*Left: White flowers purify the
blue of delphinium spires.
Above: A sprinkling of blue
hydrangeas and lush foliage.
Right: A luminous mixture of
scabious (Scabiosa), cornflowers
(Centaurea cyanus) and scented
mint (Mentha).*

the delphiniums, can emphasize this dramatic quality. A monochrome blue bunch can move from deepest cobalt to palest azure. Blue teamed with violet tends toward purple, as you can see in a bunch of anemones *(Anemone)*. Gray foliage will increase blue's brilliance; or you can sharpen violet-blues with a dash of lime-green leaf. A contrast of blue and yellow or blue and orange looks especially vivid when the colors are used in equal amounts. However, pure blue and red in equal amounts are not restful companions as they war with each other. Blue and white flowers can be emphasized by using blue-and-white china containers.

PURPLE

Pure purple is an intense hue, whose strength of color is beautifully emphasized with dark or pale green, white, blue or pink. Yellow makes the hue appear more luminous. To gauge the effect, take a simple bunch of miniature pansies (*Viola tricolor*) and set them among sprigs of golden rod (*Solidago*), trimmed short. Some purple flowers look best massed on their own, for example, violets (*Viola odorata*) are best presented in nosegays with a ring of their own deep green leaves; that way they appear just as they would when growing in the woodland.

Below: A mix of scabious (Scabiosa) with hydrangea (Hydrangea), meadow rue (Thalictrum), sea holly (Eryngium) and tolmiea (Tolmiea) leaf.

Right: Mauve tulips and common lilac (Syringa). Below: Dappled cyclamen (Cyclamen) leaves and tolmiea (Tolmiea) spill from a glazed bowl.

GREEN

Green flowers have a special impact when used in isolation or treated as accent colors in mixed groupings to enliven other hues. Sometimes, the silvery leaves of senecio *(Senecio)* or blue-green leaves of rue *(Ruta graveolens)* can highlight a green flower, but delicate green blooms can be easily flattened when combined with too much foliage. Flowers tagged "viridis" are a brilliant apple green –such as the green bells of false hellebore *(Veratum viride)* or the emerald variety of love-lies-bleeding *(Amaranthus 'Viridis')*. The guelder rose *(Viburnum opulus)* provides a subtle green accent and some flowers, such as varieties of spurge *(Euphorbia)*, are an eye-catching yellow-green. Hellebores *(Helleborus)* are a useful source of green flowers throughout the seasons, and another valuable flower is bells of Ireland *(Moluccella laevis)* which has five-sided papery bells that cluster on tall slender stalks. In midsummer, when the hues of the garden seem

vibrant, quieter green flowers bring a breath of fresh air to an interior, and in winter, when the landscape is dominated by dark evergreen foliage, green flowers can be equally lively.

Left: This low table-piece features the pineapple lily with starry clusters of flowers, bells of Ireland (Moluccella laevis), poppy (Papaver) capsules and emerald-green Amaranthus (Amaranthus 'Viridis'). Right: Large rhubarb (Rheum) leaves combine with slender iris (Iris) leaves and oak (Quercus) leaves.

WHITE

White is the color of so many beautiful flowers – waxy white gardenia *(Gardenia)*, white fragrant jasmine *(Jasminum)*, hazy white flowers of mid-summer gypsophila *(Gypsophila)* and the velvety white of the scented tobacco plant *(Nicotiana)* that gleams so exquisitely at night. The look of white blooms varies according to their texture, as well as the markings on the petals. Delicate veining in pink, gold and bronze will also influence the overall effect. Look at the Madonna lily *(Lilium candidum)* which grows so freely in country gardens: its inner trumpet is suffused with gold. White can tone down a mixed bunch or give added zest to an otherwise monotone arrangement. More boldly, you can take the lead with white, using it as the main theme. White blooms and silver-leafed plants enrich each other and white-and-green variegated leaves, for example, spotted lung-wort *(Pulmonaria)*, also make a good accompaniment. Mix these leaves with a few white roses *(Rosa)*, white lilac *(Syringa)*, sweet rocket *(Hesperis matronalis)* and

Left: Tiny lily-of-the-valley bells (Convallaria majalis) are defined by lime-green euphorbia (Euphorbia robbiae) and helle-bores (Helleborus foetidus). Right: White bells of snowflake (Leucojum) are displayed in two glass containers, the slanted stems below water level provid-ing an interesting pattern.

Above: A glass fish bowl holds anemones (Anemone), a single tulip (Tulipa) and white roses, all linked by the criss-crossing lines of stems. Dainty tolmiea (Tolmiea) leaves complete the effect.

stocks *(Matthiola)* and you will have a fragrant and informal all-white bunch. White flowers bloom throughout the year. In winter, pale snowdrops *(Galanthus nivalis)*, jonquils *(Narcissus jonquilla)* and crocuses *(Crocus)* reflect the wintry landscape. Spring brings arching boughs of cherry and pear blossom and scented lily-of-the-valley *(Convallaria majalis)*, followed by mock orange *(Philadelphus)* and cheerfu

white asters *(Aster)*. In woodlands starry white anemones *(Anemone)* and delicate heartsease *(Viola tricolor)* carpet shady walks. Likewise, you can brighten up a dark corner at home using white flowers set among dark glossy leaves.

The buttery sheen of cream flowers gives them a distinctive hue. Set magnolia *(Magnolia)* heads in a bowl, or grow creamy miniature waterlilies *(Nymphaea pygmea helvolva)* from seed, to embellish a dinner table.

Above: Lilies are trimmed to fit little pots and are set off with summery Stephanandra leaves.
Left: Arum lilies (Zantedeschia), spiralled here in a glass cylinder, are among the few flowers that are pure white. The petals are like fine paper.

MIXED

The colors in a flower arrangement should always be chosen to complement their surroundings – the wall coverings, drapes, furnishings and paintwork. Combining colors involves harmonizing or contrasting different hues. Colors are either warm or cool. The warm colors contain some yellow pigment, and include scarlet, orange, yellow-greens and yellow itself; the cool colors include some blue pigment and encompass crimson, violet, indigo, blue-green and true blue. To harmonize colors, choose blooms from within the same area of the spectrum so that each color appears to drift or blend harmoniously into its neighbor without any jarring effect. The other technique is to create an unexpected contrast by putting opposites against each other. If, for example, you set crimson against scarlet you will create a contrasting splash or "accent" color which will make a strong impact. Harmonizing colors are much easier to combine successfully than contrasting ones.

The simplest approach is to choose flowers from the same family or species. For example, stocks (*Matthiola*) bloom in cream, soft pink, lilac and mauve, all of which blend sympathetically. Common lilac (*Syringa*) also offers a

Left: A still life of blue blooms set off by dark-eyed yellow chrysanthemums (Chrysanthemum).
Right: The red ranunculus (Ranunculus) dominate this display. The fallen petals spill into a bowl scented with a few drops of rosewater.

profusion of violet, lilac and white on large sprays. Once you have chosen the basic color scheme you can deepen the effect by adding darker shades of the same hues, or lighten it by adding paler tints, or white or cream. Group paler colors together to give them emphasis. Contrasting colors demand an assured touch; experiment boldly by marrying green with red, blue with yellow or violet with orange. Contrasting hues of identical densities will war with each other, so it is far preferable to combine a light and a dark color, or a strong tone with a muted one.

Left: A hallway decorated with welcoming flowers. Old leather cases and umbrella containers are enlivened by the soft pinks of Joe Pye weed (Eupatorium), bridewort (Spiraea salicifolia) and yellow chrysanthemums (Chrysanthemum).

Above right: A tall arrangement of lilies with silver birch (Betula pendula) beside a vase, see page 6.

Right: The circular table and two vases in this display are unified by turquoise. The pink phlox (Phlox) softens the strong green foliage.

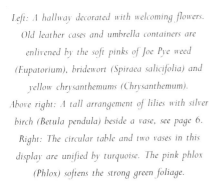

37

The Country Garden

SCENTS OF THE COUNTRY

Scent is an elusive, highly individual experience, which cannot be measured on any scale. Yet most people would agree upon the associations that scents conjure up. For example, a bowlful of sweet peas *(Lathyrus odoratus)* is enough to capture all the fragrance of a country cottage garden.

Pungent, spicy, honied, garlicky, balmy – these are just some of the adjectives that are used to evoke the scents of different flowers or leaves. Yet many scents are unique, and defy such easy description. For instance, wallflowers *(Cheiranthus)* have their own special scent, with a hint of both jasmine and orange. The scent of violets *(Viola odorata)* is more elusive: in William Shakespeare's words: "Forward, not permanent: sweet, not lasting. The perfume and suppliance of a minute." From the sensuous richness of roses *(Rosa)* and lilies *(Lilium)* to the humble charm of the simple country nosegay, scent is an integral part of the appreciation of flowers.

Left: Sweet peas (Lathyrus odoratus) are bunched simply in a fish tank, although they can also be displayed in jugs, with their tendrils and leaves.
Right: Scented flowers conjure up country walks. Fragrant roses in pastel shades are mixed with flowering mint (Mentha), sweet honeysuckle (Lonicera) and barberry (Berberis).

The rose is perhaps the flower most prized for fragrance. The famous tea scent that rose lovers enthuse about originated in China. In the early 19th century tea roses were imported to the West in the cargo holds of tea traders' vessels. They were then married with hardier varieties already established in the West and so began the long history of hybridization that yielded the modern, delicately scented hybrid

Above: Roses are romantic, their velvety blooms a traditional accompaniment to candlelit evenings.

teas. When planning an arrangement of scented roses indoors, you should take into account the room conditions, for fragrance depends on the release of essential oils, which is encouraged by a warm, humid atmosphere. If you place cut flowers in a cold room then even the most highly scented varieties will tend to disappoint.

The lily also exudes a delicious scent and, with its regal bearing and ability to last well, it is particularly popular with flower arrangers. Lilies can be tucked into bouquets as focal flowers or set alone in glass containers to be admired for their grace. Avoid using containers which are too elaborate or they will detract from the perfect flower forms. All lilies need careful handling and they are best bought or picked in bud, as they open well in water. The stems should be split and the base leaves removed. The stamens should be snipped off to prevent staining.

On a summer evening in a scented country garden a haunting mixture of fragrances fills the air. Try creating a similar blend of perfumes indoors by arranging garden flowers in mixed bunches. For example, take long stems of buddleia (*Buddleia*), broom (*Genista*), trailing honeysuckle (*Lonicera*), heliotrope (*Heliotropium peruvianum*) and night-scented stock (*Matthiola*) and arrange them in a loose spray. Some flowers smell strongest at dawn, others at dusk, and sometimes the noonday sun is needed to release the fragrant oils that tempt the butterflies and bees.

Above and below: Herbs provide an aromatic base for arrangements. Even as their flowers or leaves begin to fade, they retain their scent.

When the petals drop off then you can add them to a *potpourri* mixture. Rose petals, acacia (*Acacia dealbata*) blossom, verbena (*Verbena*) leaves, lemon balm (*Melissa officinalis*), rosemary (*Rosmarinus officinalis*) and mint (*Mentha*) are typical ingredients. Store the mixture in an airtight jar until the petals fade and the fragrance builds up, and add powdered orris root and spices to retain the sweet smell.

All sorts of aromatic herbs can be used in mixed bunches to add fragrance. Many herbs are evergreens, providing year-around foliage.

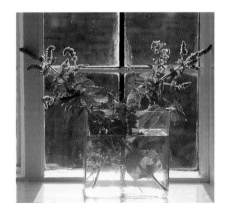

WILD & GARDEN FLOWERS

Intensive modern farming methods have made wild flowers vulnerable. However, some wild flowers are now available commercially in seed packets, thus the colors, scents and textures of the countryside migrate into the suburban garden and plants of heathland, grassland, meadows or woodland can be sown, grown and cut without fear of depleting the countryside of its natural heritage. Wild and garden flowers in arrangements bring an interior closer to nature. Traditionally, a small portion of the country garden was set aside for cutting flowers and prize blooms would be gathered and taken indoors before the summer sun rose. Favorites include blowsy peonies (*Paeonia*), tall spires of hollyhocks (*Althaea rosea*), azure delphiniums (*Delphinium*) and more retiring pansies (*Viola tricolor*). Trees and shrubs also provide useful foliage as well as flowers through the year. The yellow forsythia (*Forsythia*) brightens cold wintry days along with pussy willow (*Salix*) catkins.

Left: A heavy container of hedge snippings and licorice-scented fennel (Foeniculum vulgare).
Right: A trio dominated by foxgloves (Digitalis).

44

Berries, fruits and seed pods make attractive fall or autumn arrangements. Rosehips, renowned for their medicinal qualities, cotoneaster *(Cotoneaster)*, hawthorn *(Crataegus)* and skimmia *(Skimmia)* have decorative red fruits which lend welcome color and texture as the year starts to draw to a close, and they have the additional bonus of longevity. Juniper *(Juniperus)* and Barberry *(Berberis)* bushes

provide plentiful black fruits and the pure ivory white of the snowberry (*Symphoricarpos*), set upon a tangle of black twigs, is equally eye-catching.

Free growth and elegant outlines distinguish ferns and grasses. Ferns fall in graceful arches when combined in floral decorations and look particularly effective mixed in large masses in green arrangements. Ornamental grasses with their pearl-like seeds set along arched stems are responsive to the slightest breeze; try interspersing their delicate, wispy forms with blooms and foliage to give the whole display a tremulous quality. For arrangements that suggest the wilderness beyond our windows, snip bunches of green from hedgerows. Collect lacy cow parsley (*Anthriscus*), the leathery little galax (*Galax*) ruff and trails of wandering ivy (*Hedera*). Look too for lady's mantle (*Alchemilla*), whose umbrella-shaped leaf is designed to hold a drop of water in its central cup.

Left: Flowering shrubs are all too often cut for the flowers rather than the leaves. However, here the foliage in many shades of green predominates.
Above: A loose massed bunch in a glass cube.
Right: A wild spray spills from a glass goblet.

47

FOLIAGE

The beauty of leaves is scarcely appreciated out of doors but, once brought inside, each leaf can be considered for its individual qualities. Foliage may exhibit a multitude of colorings such as cream and white variegations; golden stripes and white splashings; plum, maroon or chocolate-brown patterns in horse-shoe shapes, stripes or dots. As well as interesting markings, leaves come in an array of bright hues including glowing yellow, deep purple, tawny bronze, blue-gray or silver, as well as a host of true greens. Some leaf shapes curl protectively around a bunch of flowers in a simple nosegay, and others come in great sprays or

Below left: This arrangement shows contrasts within the blue-gray spectrum; it has a smoky subtlety.

Below right: Grasses picked from a wild garden offer variegations and textures that draw the eye.

Right: A lavish bunch of massed knotweed (Polygonum) in a richly ornamented spherical vase.

branches and fill big containers. Foliage changes color with the turning seasons so that fall or autumn offers a palette of deep red, crimson, scarlet and amber which can be set off to good effect among evergreen and silvery silken grasses. Place large sprays in copper containers or baskets, anchored at the base with pebbles. Creepers add accent color to a simple bunch of late-summer flowers. More than fill-ins for flowers, foliage offers a richness of color, line and pattern.

Left: A light and delicate mixture of green and copper beech (Fagus).
Above left: A glass cylinder holds shapely branches of whitebeam (Sorbus aria).
Above right: House plants can be a useful addition to fresh cut flowers.
This grouping evokes a watery landscape of tall reeds and mossy banks.

The Art of Composition

CONTAINERS

Containers transform flowers. They affect the color and the texture of the bloom, as well as that indefinable quality, mood. Designing with flowers is the alliance between container and plant material. Flowers in glass containers take on the clarity of the glass, as the contrast between the colors is highlighted and sharpened by the green stems showing through it. Make use of single-stem vases in clear glass. Intended for buds, they are perfect containers for open blooms or tiny posies. In contrast, the texture of a ceramic container makes a bolder contribution to an arrangement, and plain earthenware glazes, alabaster or marble will grace

Below left: Wicker baskets lend themselves to long flower heads which tumble out in arching spires.
Below right: Bare boards make an unaffected background for a basketful of fresh country flowers.
Right: A rustic basket, with a waterproof lining, makes a charmingly informal flower container.

Above: A free, informal bunch of hedgerow pickings is framed by the curving handle of a glass basket; longer stems grace the taller goblet. Criss-cross the stems so that they form a web to support each other.

Right: Flowers picked in bud have a longer life indoors. It is always a pleasure to see the buds gradually opening until they develop into full-blown blooms. I picked lilies (Lilium longiflorum), roses and eustoma (Eustoma) and placed them with bamboo in shallow glass bowls and a pair of small glass jars. At the budding stage the leaves dominate. Then, when the flowers start to open, color is more important than line, so producing a summery bouquet.

most flowers. Plain, vibrantly colored vases are useful for complementing flowers with strong hues, while patterned glazes should be carefully chosen to blend comfortably with your blooms. The gleam of metal makes a subdued base for flowers, to suit all sorts of settings. The color of metal affects the tones of the flowers. For instance, warm shades are cooled by silver and strike a grand note. Bronze and copper give a warmer glint, and even a tin pail or galvanized metal watering can makes a sturdy but charming container, given a coat of paint.

There is also a host of less orthodox flower holders such as wicker baskets, old medicine bottles, household pots and even fish tanks. There are no limits to the possibilities, for a true scavenger can turn almost anything to use.

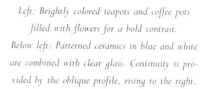

Left: Brightly colored teapots and coffee pots filled with flowers for a bold contrast.
Below left: Patterned ceramics in blue and white are combined with clear glass. Continuity is provided by the oblique profile, rising to the right.

Above right: Floor-standing containers filled with flowers can transform the dullest corner. In this hallway I have used plumes of bocconia (Macleaya), green bells of Ireland (Moluccella laevis), leaves and berries of St John's wort (Hypericum) and white scented tuberoses (Polianthes) are the right scale for a sturdy vase.

Above: A dark cast-iron bowl suggests strength and resilience and needs a delicate combination of flowers in fresh-looking colors to contest that impression. Here, fresh flat-top hydrangeas (Hydrangea) in pink, blue and white offer a charming antidote to the severity of the matte black container.

INDEX

GENERAL

acacia 43
alstroemeria 15
amaranthus 28
anemone 13, 25, 27, 32
arum lily 33
artichoke 17
aster 33
azalea 15, 17

barberry 41, 46-7
basil, purple 13
baskets 54-5, 57
beech 50
bells of Ireland 10, 28, 28, 58
berries 46
blue flowers 22-5, 22-5
bocconia 58
bridewort 16, 36
broom 43
buddleia 43
buttercup 18

carnation 13, 21
chrysanthemum 34, 36
cider gum 14
containers 54-7, 54-9
cornflower 22, 25
cotoneaster 46
cow parsley 47
crab apple 13
crocosmia 21
crocus 33
crown imperial 21
cyclamen 13, 26

daffodil 18, 19
dahlia 13, 14
day lily 18
delphinium 22-5, 22, 24, 44
dogwood 20

euphorbia 30
eustoma 57

false hellebore 28
fennel 44
fern 47
foliage 20, 48-51, 48-51
forget-me-not 22
forsythia 44
foxglove 45

galax 47
gardenia 30
gentian 22
geranium 13, 20
gerbera 10, 12, 14
gladiolus 14
golden rod 18, 26
grasses 17, 47, 48, 51
green flowers 28-31, 28-31
guelder rose 22, 28
gypsophila 30

hawthorn 46
heartsease 33
heather 17
heliotrope 43
hellebore 28, 30
herbs 43, 43
hollyhock 44
honeysuckle 41, 43
hosta 7, 20
hyacinth 17
hydrangea 16, 17, 23, 25, 26, 59

iris 18, 29
ivy 20, 47

jasmine 20, 30
Joe Pye weed 16, 36
jonquil 33
juniper 46-7

lady's mantle 47
lavender 14
lemon balm 43
lilac 14, 30, 34-7
lily 7, 21, 33, 37, 40, 42, 57
lily-of-the-valley 30, 33
love-in-a-mist 16, 22
love-lies-bleeding 28
lungwort 30
lupin 22

Madonna lily 30
magnolia 33
marigold 21
meadow rue 26
Michaelmas daisy 14, 17
mimosa 18, 18
mint 25, 41, 43
mixed colors 34-7, 34-7
mock orange 33
montbretia 20

pansy 26, 44
peony 13, 17, 44
Peruvian lily 21
phlox 37
pineapple lily 28
pink flowers 14-17
poppy 13, 28
potpourri 43
primrose 21
primula 18
purple flowers 26-9 -
pussy willow 44

ranunculus 7, 35
red flowers 10-13, 10-13
rhubarb 29
rose 10-13, 11, 13, 14, 18, 30, 32, 40, 41, 42, 42, 43, 57
rosehip 46

rosemary 43
rudbeckia 21
rue 28

sage 13
St John's wort 10, 18, 58
scabious 22, 25, 26
scents 40-3
sea holly 26
senecio 17, 21, 28
silver birch 37
skimmia 46
smoke tree 21
snapdragon 18
snowberry 47
snowdrop 33
snowflakes 31
spurge 17, 28
stock 17, 33, 34, 43
sunflower 18
sweet pea 17, 40, 40
sweet rocket 30

tobacco plant 21, 30
tolmiea 26, 32
tuberose 58
tulip 13, 32

variegated foliage 20
verbena 43
violet 26, 40

wallflower 20, 40
waterlily 33
weigela 13, 21
white flowers 30-3, 30-3
whitebeam 22, 51
wild flowers 44-7, 44-7

yarrow 18
yellow flowers 18-21

LATIN

Acacia dealbata 18, 18, 43
Achillea 18
Alchemilla 47
Alstroemeria 15, 21
Althaea rosea 44
Amaranthus 'Viridis' 28, 28
Anemone 13, 25, 27, 32, 33
Anthriscus 47
Antirrhinum majus 18
Aster 14, 17, 33

Berberis 41, 46
Betula pendula 37
Buddleia 43

Calendula officinalis 21
Centaurea cyanus 22, 25
Cheiranthus 20, 40
Chrysanthemum 34, 36
Convallaria majalis 30, 33
Cornus 20
Cotinus 21
Cotoneaster 46
Crataegus 46
Crocosmia 21
Crocus 33
Cyclamen 13, 27
Cynara scolymus 17

Dahlia 13, 14
Delphinium 22, 22, 24, 44
Dianthus 13, 21
Digitalis 45

Erica 17

Eryngium 26
Eucalyptus gunnii 14
Eupatorium 36
    Eupatorium purpureum 16
Euphorbia 17, 28
    Euphorbia robbiae 7, 30
Eustoma 57

Fagus 50
Foeniculum vulgare 44
Forsythia 44
Fritillaria imperialis 21

Galanthus nivalis 33
Galax 47
Gardenia 30
Genista 43
Gentiana 22
Gerbera 10, 12, 14
Gladiolus 14
Gypsophila 30

Hedera 20, 47
Helianthus 18
Heliotropium peruvianum 43
Helleborus 28
    Helleborus foetidus 30
Hemerocallis 18
Hesperis matronalis 30
Hosta 7, 20
Hyacinthus 17
Hydrangea 16, 17, 23, 25, 26, 59
Hypericum 10, 18, 58

Ilex 20
Iris 18, 29

Jasminum 20, 30

Juniperus 46
Lathyrus odoratus 17, 40, 40
Lavandula 14
Leucojum 31
Lilium 21, 40
    Lilium candidum 30
    Lilium longiflorum 57
    Lilium 'Peach Blush' 7
Lonicera 41, 43
Lupinus 22

Macleaya 58
Magnolia 33
Malus 13
Matthiola 17, 33, 34, 43
Melissa officinalis 43
Mentha 25, 41, 43
Moluccella laevis 10, 28, 28, 58
Montbretia 20
Myosotis 22

Narcissus 18, 19
    Narcissus jonquilla 33
Nicotiana 21, 30
Nigella damascena 16, 22
Nymphaea pygmea helvola 33

Ocimum basilicum 13

Paeonia 13, 17, 44
Papaver 13, 28
Pelargonium 13, 20
Philadelphus 33
Phlox 37
Polianthes 58
Polygonum 49
Primula auricula 18
    Primula vulgaris 21

Pulmonaria 30

Quercus 29

Ranunculus 7, 35
    Ranunculus acris 18
Rheum 29
Rhododendron 15, 17
Rosa 18, 30, 40
    Rosa 'Floribunda' 14
Rosmarinus officinalis 43
Rudbeckia 21
Ruta graveolens 28

Salix 44
Salvia 13
Scabiosa 22, 25, 26
Senecio 17, 21, 28
Skimmia 46
Solidago 18, 26
Sorbus aria 22, 51
Spiraea salicifolia 16, 36
Stephanandra 33
Symphoricarpos 47
Syringa 14, 30, 34-7

Thalictrum 26
Tolmiea 26, 32
Tulipa 13, 32

Veratrum viride 28
Verbena 43
Viburnum opulus 22, 28
Viola odorata 26, 40
    Viola tricolor 26, 33, 44

Weigela 13, 21

Zantedeschia 33

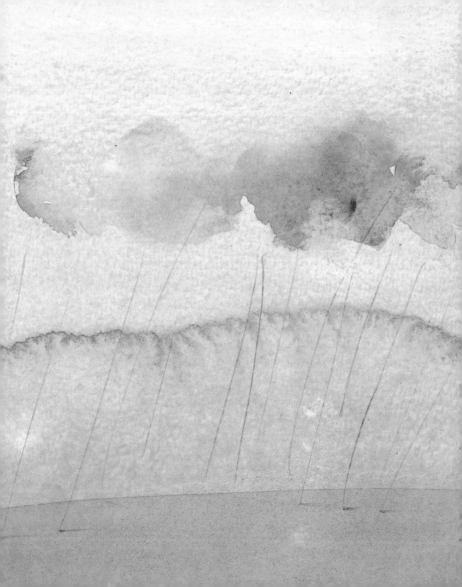